RIDING MY TRICYCLE

RIDING MY TRICYCLE

Poetry of Dreams and Visions

Ann M. DeVenezia

Copyright © 2006 by Ann M. DeVenezia

Library of Congress Number: 2005910706
ISBN :   Softcover   1-4257-0480-8

All rights reserved. No part of this book may be reproduced or transmitted in any form or by any means, electronic or mechanical, including photocopying, recording, or by any information storage and retrieval system, without permission in writing from the copyright owner.

Author photograph by Richard F. DeVenezia

Printed in the United States of America

To order additional copies of this book, contact:
Xlibris Corporation
1-888-795-4274
www.Xlibris.com
Orders@Xlibris.com
32671

Contents

Dream Your Route/Map Your Vision 9
Haying 10
Tractor 11
Still Playing Checkers 12
Cemetery Cave 13
Moments of Horror 14
Autumn Dream 15
The Long Way 16
A Visit from My Mother 17
Nighttime Flying 18
Sense and Nonsense 19
Dogs in the Canary Islands 20
Dog Whisperer 21
Half Remembered/Half Forgotten 22
Where I Sleep 23
The Ogre's Reply 24
Two Hours a Day 25
Eyes Shut Tight 26
Half Asleep 27
Sleeping and Waking 28
Eyes Straight Ahead 29
Carnival Night 30
Dream Scene 32
Dreams in Color 33
Nighttime Rain 34
Hide and Seek 35
Riding My Tricycle 36
Waking Up 38
A Room of Her Own 39
Bag Lady 40
Dream with a Theme 41
Look at Me 42

Signs along Life's Highway	43
Taking a Shortcut	45
Detour	46
Master of Deceit	47
Midnight Shopping	48
To a Winged Spirit	49
Ice Maiden: Child of Sacrifice	50
The General's Report	51
News of the Crash	52
Walpurgis Stew	53
Free Spirits	54
Sonnet of Delight	55
Death of Romance	56
Spa Night	57
Thunder	58
Comic Strips	59
Our Son's Odyssey	61
The Way Things Work	63
World Trade Center: September 11, 2001	64
Words from Afar	66
Acknowledgments	67

IN MEMORIAM

Mary M. Lupardi
(1905-1984)

Anthony P. Lupardi
(1901-1974)

Dream Your Route/Map Your Vision

Like islanders who create three-dimensioned maps,
weave pliable sticks and twine for your memory cage
Think hard while you circle the vines round each other

Into the map's hollow core, place talismans
venerated tokens of the land you plan on leaving
a stone, a seed, a leaf, the ring your mother wore

Carry this worldly orb wherever you go
Put it on a candle-lit table in a new home
Implore its strength each night before sleep

Insert a sea shell, grain of sand, lock of hair,
a trusty key, the pipe your father puffed
Take your totems to the next destination

Use this guide and you will live your life
to eternity, above and beyond imagination,
landscape and memory intertwined.

Haying

In the autumn of the year
on our way to upstate New York
my eyes wander the meadows

where giant marshmallows lie in rows
silage hidden by stretched white plastic
mower and conveyor rolling to other fields

Virgin pillows call cows to bed
in red barns nestled near blue towers
housing hay for winter's cattle

Who sleeps in the hay
could be Little Boy Blue
his horn flung aside

or young lovers
arms and legs tangled
hayseed in their hair.

Tractor

The rusted Farmall
no longer red
rests on discouraged treads
wheels chained to the ground

When I reach the corroded seat
my hands are black with grime
and my legs hurt from the climb
but I see the fields again

ripe for the cutting
a hay wagon here for the haul
my father holding his pitchfork
in high salute.

Still Playing Checkers

My father and I sit touching knees to knees
my legs much shorter than his yet
the board balances on an old wine keg

He jumps my reds with his blacks
as doubled discs march forward and back
sweeping my singles to the ground

It still feels good when I see my reds jump
his single blacks and hear myself shout
        King Me! King Me!

Cemetery Cave

Before I entered the cave
I knocked a fat crow off my shoulder

Inside I found nothing but damp earth
split by a thin muddy stream

a dry wall
a hand outlined in red ochre

the spot where a sharp stone made its marks
with a cutting edge

Out from the dark
I lay on my back to see the light

Two thin crows flew from atop a concrete cross
and began to peck at my chest.

Moments of Horror

Snakes, helicopters, and cliffs;
my heart beats faster at the thought
of escalators, hurricanes, robbers,
but, most of all, I fear being alone

When I hear the muffled tapping,
I think it's a burglar at the door;
with no one else at home
I lie down and hug the floor

Footfalls shake the porch,
force me to face fear;
my hands grip the ledge
as I stare above the sill

In the dark, I spy a shadowy form,
bulky tools in gloved hands
I know not why he sneaks away
leaving me cold as stone.

Autumn Dream

Sad leaves
falling down the hole of memory
choking the way to forbidden

where we pry the eyes
of three kittens in the shed
your large hand on my arm

candlelight casting shadows
on the closed door
till it swings open

Silence fills the empty spaces
as we stare at each other
eyes sliding over naked bodies.

The Long Way

I live in the land of the dead
digging up bones
with no meat left

I leave the living flesh
for ancient risks
fiery thrills

I go alone for sneaky tricks
astride a beam behind tall pines
No words roll off my tongue

Riding a spotted pony
I dodge a tethered bull
taking the long way home

Right or wrong
making not a sound
I continue round and round.

A Visit from My Mother

She died twenty years ago today
but last night she came to visit
gray hair and her special smile
soft brown eyes behind tortoise glasses

We sit on the top back porch step
of the old house in which I was born
seventy years earlier
close as we were that morning

She holds a *Woman's Day* magazine
in one hand, her rosary beads in the other
asks me how I am feeling
if I'm happy

I tell her I'm fine but always tired
what with worrying about the children
and writing poetry to be published
meeting friends for lunch and chatter

The telephone rings but we won't answer;
this is our time together, seldom a chance
to talk anymore with her gone and me here
I ask her how she's doing

She's doing well, with Dad, her brothers, sisters,
whole family, except the five of us and our spouses
We hug and she fades from view
leaving me alone on the stoop with memories.

Nighttime Flying

Dad says never go near the dark stairs
on the way to the bathroom; feel for the wall
far from a chair placed like a gate

Mom warns I will fall from the second floor
break my bones the way my sister did
but she did not have this flying gift

When I stretch aloft and step into the void
I soar through the deep stairwell
down and up on currents of air

Next morning I teach my other sister
so in case of a fire in the bedroom
we can throw our mattress to the ground

stand on the window sill and jump
land together in a joyful heap
a leap through time and space.

Sense and Nonsense

A cow, two kittens, and a suitcase
my talking on the phone while leaving home

Going for a swim with two daughters
while their father watches us dive

My sister stores her tablecloths so high
on a skinny shelf outside on the porch

she uses a ladder to climb up to get them
jumps down onto a bridge table by my feet

I tell her it's dangerous to go to such extremes
for keeping things in place and neat

Old friends usually not seen appear and reappear
wonder where I have been for so many years

The brakes on my car fail and
I fly alone over a waterfall.

Dogs in the Canary Islands

Last night I had a dream
about strange dogs

Sharp teeth, bare ribs
they float free

I poke at one with a stick
it turns into a heap of rags

I reach for another and
it flies through a wall

Other big brownish dogs
chew on my bones

Fat canaries peck my hair
as I run for the stairs.

Dog Whisperer

Teeth bared, the mastiff scratches,
snaps, and bites the tall man
the one with calm hands

The man holds this terror close
strokes both ears and holds back fangs
rubs the chest of the beast

Others growl, sniff, stick snouts
at cowering crowds of fans
watching from behind barriers

The man again and again
leans to a fearsome face
his mouth at a dog's ear

Whispering words of gentle gibberish
he handles huge paws; one by one, he sends
these animals to their canine dreams.

Half Remembered/Half Forgotten

Peering through quartered glass,
I spy jackets half wet/half dry, raised on thin sticks
second-story high

Just moments ago
children were here kicking balls
in half wet/half dry snow

What's the name emblazoned on their coats
letters on each side of front zippers
ending with something like " . . . acketeers"?

I'm here in a deserted house
with one man and our dreams
the sky opening behind us

Last night he dreamt his father came to visit him
first time in forty-three years
They were making wine after all that time

My dream the usual behind closed doors
holding us in against storm and strangers
in a place we don't belong.

Where I Sleep

An empty ferry boat
Loaded with rattling rocks

Sails away from shore.
I swim to catch the rail.

Watching the river's flow
I mark the miles deep.

This golden fairy ship's
Wooden paddles slice the air.

On my bunk I turn and turn
Beneath twisted velvet sheets

Caught by currents
Whirling in a dream.

The Ogre's Reply

In the forest, lions and tigers
monkeys, mice, and deer
converse with me

I dine with dwarfs and giants
wear lace and silver, lounge on couches
strum my golden sitar for them

I wear a coned hat set high on blond tresses;
two bags near my red velvet feet
hold songs not for sale

I play with trinkets and toys
float through thick pine branches
wave a wand above the ground

Please be patient while I think;
we must watch for elves and imps
small things that spell disaster

When a stranger courts me with kisses
puts more rings on my fingers and toes
I leave my land and follow him

In the desert, after he shouts curses
beats me and laughs
I cry for help

Tiny bells on silken threads
summon only a monster who says
I must stay where I am.

Two Hours a Day

and fast without thinking till my pen clogs
with no hills or valleys
like driving through Kansas

then a large beast jumps out
spewing smoke and steam in the dust
from the place where three roads meet

a voice repeats in my ear
   Kill the beast or be eaten
so I run it over, keep going

that wasn't two hours, more like two minutes
my husband snoring on the Monet-flowered sheets
me trying to silence a cacophonous waterfall

I listen to my nib scratching the surface
describe Dostoevsky's earrings behind the door
Gogol's three flies floating in red wine

the Venetian leather wallet on the bedside table
shows signs of wear, but two brass knobs click shut
after I insert my eyeglasses and pen—Amen.

Eyes Shut Tight

It took all day to thread the needle
poking a waxed tip through the eye
At last the end slipped through

The late night picture show spinning
on the inside of my eyes shut tight
showed odd rug pieces pressed to fit

The man in my house shouted
he had a puzzle to solve
never enough time to do it

Gypsies arrived looking to sell
baptismal records and bedroom slippers
used my perfumes and powders

I chased them away with barking dogs
braced our home with bars and chains
electronic eyes to scan the skies

In the morning they were gone
leaving a trail of tin cups and dishes
red ribbons and tambourines.

Half Asleep

All day
I wear an airy blue blouse
yellow sun and brass buttoned
on the back a map
> *The Most Beautiful Country in the World*

In cities like Rome and Pisa
bells tower next to baptistries
heel aligned with an island
kicked off the toe
of this elongated boot

All night
funny sayings from Italy
cling to the sheets
knot my hair
> *Venga qua*
> *Setaca*

I creep across glowing embers
search the broken bridge
crawl down river banks

At dawn
I wake to olive trees near empty houses
fingers to their lips
> *Don't say that*
> *Don't even think it.*

Sleeping and Waking

Fish foot-dance in the streets
Girls web-walk to the streams
Birds dressed like clowns
hop under the banyan trees

A red rose blooms
among the autumn leaves
and wet snow falls
on a summer day

In this misty wonderland of dreams
we waltz to the sounds of Strauss
arms wrapped round each other
bodies swaying to a steady beat

When I awoke, as hoped
I found a tiny clown suit
a bouquet of red roses
and you in my bed.

Eyes Straight Ahead

Molten lead bubbles in the abyss
far below my rocky precipice and
I walk along the cliff's high ledge

Like an amateur tightrope walker
I place one foot in front of the other
cringing without looking down

I scan a dark sky and take a deep breath
quicken slow steps to a hop and skip
afraid of crags yet no longer bent

My back pressed against the wall
I avoid careening stones flung cross my path
stride to the end of a dusty trail

smile at what I have done.

Carnival Night

Was it an elevator? Who was there?
Two young ladies in spangled tights next to me
in a space wide enough for twelve elephants

Faster and faster we ascended
the huge room rising till stars appeared
viewed through a glass roof

As we gazed into the night
a metal bar swung across our bodies
a Ferris wheel rocking us into the void

Suddenly the floor descended to the street
the girls racing to their high wire act
I tried to get out, but two clowns pushed me back

Complaining loudly, I made them let me go
paying to buy lifetime tickets, big bargain
for lovers of fantastic fun and adventures

The sideshows touted a bearded lady with red hair
a giant of a man over eight feet tall, married to
a woman with no body from the rib cage down

They told me they planned on moving to a town in Florida
populated by freaks of nature and retired sideshow acts
where they could live in peace from curious customers

I ducked under their flap and slipped into a new tent
alone with a dog and a goat that greeted me by name
but a rowdy crowd gathered, shouting for more

The charmer appeared in white loin cloth and turban;
from the floor a cobra raised its head, and soon
the ground was covered with slithering snakes.

Dream Scene

On the night of the day
my great niece was born
I lie in bed

feeling the scab on my lip
formed after eating fried fish
straight from bubbling oil

As I think about Emma and
how she shares my father's birthday
I become lost in a trance

Our yard looks cramped
like the one next door
ready for a spectacular show

Small boys dressed like Napoleon
ride tall horses painted gold
at the head of a packed parade

Exotic strangers in black
search the announcer's purse
find ticket stubs and coins

Our family holds free passes
tells others to buy their own
and leave us alone

I touch my scab
till it falls off
leaving a bloody trail.

Dreams in Color

I used to dream in technicolor
till scenery turned black and white
at times gray or beige, murky waters

Where have all the reds and greens gone?
Why this fading life for husband, wife
daughters and sons, the web undone?

No more till death do us part
like Robert and Elizabeth Browning
growing old together, the best yet to be

Leaves fall, then twigs and branches
the family tree a victim of stormy weather
When the teacher assigns an ancestor chart

whose progeny will have pages large enough?
Grandchildren wonder, "Who am I?"
Grandparents ask, "What can we do?"

When will I dream in color again?

Nighttime Rain

Scenes splash on my pillow
raining beyond a black umbrella
drenching my brain with images

Friends, strangers, lovers congregate
for a few hours, meeting together
in curious and unexpected ways

We picnic at the beach, some eating
stuffed chickens, mashed potatoes, string beans
others feasting on fried steaks, yellow corn, melons

An old green blanket is spread wide
near high waves, covering the gritty sand
where we all lie about: brothers, sisters, in-laws

We do not speak nor laugh; we eat with our hands
scoop food, use no dishes nor spoons
When I awake, for fear of loss, I do not wash my hair

Shaking loose the scenes, I write what I remember
each night awaiting a new hurricane of words
looking for images wrapped in red cellophane.

Hide and Seek

Wooly sheep, a mama ewe,
buffalo, and deer follow me
to my hiding place

behind a heavy circular disc
metal burnished greenish-gray
resting near a two-story house

I sneak inside through a private door
to where people start to dress for dinner
adults and children getting ready

Only I can find the hidden rooms
behind a long wall and secret entry
barely used but frequently visited

a whole suite with bedrooms and baths
around each bend spacious dens
resplendent with couches and cushions

velvet draperies at the windows
plush carpets on the floors
all for me, rent free

Here I wander from noon to night
locking the doors and windows
not another soul in my space

Only I can maneuver this maze
gaze into the silver-framed mirrors
seek reflections of the future.

Riding My Tricycle

When two or so, I travel far from home,
sitting on the seat of a rusty, three-wheeled vehicle,
without moving, gripping the handle bars.

Sue, the tired doll, quiet on the grass, leans by a rickety chair;
with her plaster face, arms, and legs, a cotton-filled body,
blue-checkered dress, she stares into space through glassy eyes.

Spike, the whitish mongrel, stops near our small corroded wagon,
and three black kittens blink at the sight of my motionless feet,
greenhouses for roses and tall chimney steady in the background.

If I had that trike today, I'd ride it directly into a cloudless sky,
soaring upside down and downside up, smiling the whole time.
Perched perfectly still, I'd fly to the moon, visit all planets,

zoom back to earth, park on the roof, a ready space shuttle,
no doors or windows blocking easy access to sea, earth and sky,
all else moving round me while I pause in the atmosphere.

I'd milk the cows, hands resting against warm udders,
aiming pure, vanilla streams straight into a shiny bucket.
Where the blue heron's trident footprint leads, I'd follow its tracks,

taking off and landing safely on an ebony lake, without Icarian wings.
With skis attached, I'd skim over water, or submerge, a submarine,
staring through periscope at whales, dolphins, and toothy sharks.

What makes three so special: tricycles, a trinity, flowers arranged
in odd numbers, starting with three for balance and beauty.
All on a tripod: the farmer's stool, artist's easel, astronomer's eye.

When I am old, a cane will do for my three-legged way,
traveling among dreams, scenes, and reality: parts of a triptych,
populated by people and creatures I encounter while sleeping.

Waking Up

When I awake in a cold cell
at Saint Marguerite's Retreat House
I am a kid again, asleep in my clothes
my father's heavy coat thrown over me

or a teenager on a narrow bed
in the attic of an old Dutch farmhouse
tall pine scratching and sighing
at my thick glazed window

Yet when I look out the latticed casement
my breath making a fog on the glass
I am transported to England or France
at an abbey or chateau, surprised

at the manor's whitewashed arches
marching across the greensward,
drawing me from deep dreams
to reality.

A Room of Her Own

Matilda unlocks the door
walks in and slams it behind her
hangs up her coat and cane
shut in with favorite things

Her pet frog leaps at her
croaks he is friend and lover
Suction cup feet attach to her chest
as she quickly kisses the prince

He lights her world with joy
under an enormous glass chandelier
The breeze twinkles long crystals
flutters blue and white chintz curtains

She waters drooping plastic lilies in pots
Three concrete gnomes in red hats grin and laugh
Removing a gold ring from her nose
she lies down for the night in a narrow bed.

Bag Lady

Wreaths hang on the doors
holly winds round the poles

She knows holidays are near
by songs in the street

children singing with mothers
red bows on their coats

Solo, she walks the paths
from bench to bench

A picture in her bag
lies hidden beneath scraps

white picket fence
daffodils under birches

roses over the gate
two people on the porch

She digs for it and then
buries the photo again.

Dream with a Theme

Recurring roses appear within shiny glass cases and
aromas from large petaled yellow blooms permeate the air
Red Better Times in vases abide side by side with whites and pinks
Alone, I sit on the floor bathed in perfume by the slightly ajar door
yet I wait and worry about the guard who will chase me away
since I became lost in the halls following a solo walk to the restroom

My husband and two old friends find me in an endless flower shop
where countless rows of roses grow and blossom under glass
An immense array of lush tropical growth appears in tiers
along grand marble staircases that lead to a cool flowing river
My nose is red and hands chilled, but my body breathes heat
as I stretch on the ground watching this eternal parade of roses

with Shirley who wears a white blouse and sits on a pile of baled straw
Her slim blue skirt matches prissy blue gloves and black leather shoes
Charles, her husband, in a brown suit, remains across the street
seated on piles of bricks next to two scruffy boys in checkered knickers
I do not recall what I wear and my husband has disappeared
When I awake he may return with arms full of roses.

Look at Me

I pick up the newspaper
from the end of my driveway and
look around to see who's watching

Maybe William Carlos Williams
will see me in my housecoat
and write an ode of admiration

Will he or anyone else notice
and write a poem about me
or will I have to script my own?

I'm lonely, oh so lonely
a shadow on the wall
turning, turning like a grayish fog

When I return to my scribbling
I hear myself shouting, shouting
for your attention.

Signs along Life's Highway

Limited sight: keep left, keep right
I dreamt we slept in a golden car
blue slippers on our feet
songs to be sung on our tongues
silently gliding uphill and down

We woke to a multicolored world
of painted eggs playing on gay tambourines
holding hands as they danced on stage
round and round a red rose tree
blossoms turned white while they spun

I dreamt a naked infant lay on my bed
warm, real, perfectly formed
except for one missing arm
That morning I read in the *Times*
of laundered Cambodian babies,
not bathed, powdered, or hugged

Prime infants for sale to strangers
two hundred dollars to the mother
her price spent on food for others
three thousand to the broker
for cars, dinners, more luxuries

I dreamt a stranger's revolving body
spurted blood on my white bedroom rug
as he gushed red from nose and mouth
This morning I read in the *Ledger*
a suicide bomber said, "It's beautiful to kill and be killed."

People as purple as afternoon shadows
orange as the setting sun
we rode round and round the rotary
a dead end street with no outlet
till we disappeared in a light gray fog.

Taking a Shortcut

On the road from Piermont to Beech,
we see the open space in a dense woods;
I follow my firstborn son's call of Let's Go

The last time we were here, the path
was overgrown and full of stones
Now the way is smooth, no more logs and stumps

A woman rocking on the porch of an old house
points to a fork in the road and hollers
The Waterfall Comes Up Soon

Wishing for beautiful sights
we take the road she shows
eschewing entries to caves

Oceans of bluebells fill the fields
dotted with buttercups and lavender
pulling us deeper into a Monet painting

till spying a rope bridge, I yell No Way
having forgotten trying the unknown
can lead to deep holes and chasms

Only a few wooden steps and no rails
so I pull back and stay put to my son's
Why Not

I clearly respond Not Today
I'd rather escape from sleep to reality
than stay in danger-laden dreams.

Detour

On the way to work with a friend,
in my sedan, we spy a detour sign
only five minutes from the factory
but we get lost next to a stone house
nuns singing an ode to joy

An arm reaches in the window
fingers turning up the radio's sound
someone saying she thought
we'd rather not hear their voices
We ask for directions and start again

Bulldozers and trucks block the road
tearing down a farmhouse and barns
throwing boulders and lumber in our path
We back up, rev the motor, full speed ahead
going over the top of debris till stuck

Locked in a room with no phones
we find bouquets of roses with thorns
bunches of daisies, lilies, and ferns
To cheers from the construction gang
we search for doors out of this scary dream.

Master of Deceit

The tall Fagin figure has a short gray beard
and he teaches young boys how to steal
He drives a battered station wagon
Town and Country with fake wooden panels

My spouse and I amble along a macadam road
see a boy I recognize from having bumped into him
The lad holds my husband's wallet till he gives it up
to the middle-aged man in the driver's seat

This urchin rushes back the way we had come
looking for another pocket to pick for the master
I run to the front of the vehicle, catch a D and a three
jot down a license number for the cops

The driver starts to chase me and I lose my husband
At an open door I run in and slam it behind me
amazed to arrive in a castle-like mansion
The dowager is dead in her tower bedroom

leaving the butler, the mailman, and the maid as suspects
plus a stranger dressed in spectacles and suspenders
When the police arrive, one of them looks slightly familiar
the same height and beard as the Fagin I fear.

Midnight Shopping

As soon as I enter the store
I see what I want for our front door
a carved creation by an unknown craftsman

Six teak wood slats tied with golden threads
dangle one below the other, from shortest to longest
on each, hand-painted scenes and a child's name

Filigree of flowers and deer flicker in the sunlight
delicate purple iris near yellow daffodils
tiny green ferns curled like fiddle heads

Stags, does, and fawns romp on narrow lawns
I reach for my purse, but through some delay
phones ringing, doors slamming, I don't get to pay

I leave empty-handed, return again and again
If by day I see that work of art once more
without a question, I will quickly buy.

To a Winged Spirit

I stare from my Arizona cliff to yours
surprised at how you gaze at me
quiet sentry by a dark splotch of water

Preening your shining, ebony feathers
will you answer my many questions?
Were you here when Anasazi scratched rocks?

Were you there pecking at bloodied bodies
searching uniforms when men fought
in Italy, Germany, Russia, Japan?

I swear some of you swarmed posts by cornfields
watching the scarecrow's every move
ready to devour a New York farmer's crop

More flew above yellow wheat in France
startled by a sound from Van Gogh's gun
as his paint box and he fell to the ground

Were you the one sitting on a bust of Athena
tap-tapping at Poe's shuttered casement
or was it your raven cousin?

I would lengthen my litany
but you've flown straight to a blue sky
summoned by your mate's angry call.

Ice Maiden: Child of Sacrifice

In the high Andes white plumes
atop her peak-shaped head
bravely fly against a topaz sky

Propped on an icy perch she leans south
small leather slipper clasped in one hand
soft alpaca cape round her shoulders

Two others and she, not quite thirteen
grip gifts of tiny golden and silver llamas
sea shells and dried meat for the journey

Gently buried under stones and snow
the drowsy playmates wait in the chill air
groggy from sacrificial drugs and corn liquor

Empty-handed, parents, porters and priests
descend the steep mountain to fertile lands
prepared for more praying and plowing

She awakes from her stupor
shivers and swallows hard
resigned to the sacred duty

Here she rests five hundred years
till diggers discover their ancestors' aerie
eighty pounds of cloth and mummified bones

They cradle their precious cargo
heavy through the thin air to Salta
for generations to cherish and admire.

The General's Report

Black hawks circle the sky
and men imitate their flight
in color of choppers going down

Natives of the town swarm
to capture grounded pilots
no longer shining in the sun

Through alleys and streets
jeeps seek the fallen birds
snatching them from enemy fire

More Black Hawks rotate rescues
finding nothing but entrails and
helmets blown off with their heads

Brilliant shafts dance among the bodies
beneath the Hawk-filled skies
awaiting night's arrival

Through night-filtering goggles
the earth turns green again
clear as bright summer.

News of the Crash

That was no Icarus that tumbled out of the sky
in Hasbrouck Heights the other day.
A four-seater crashed on its way from Virginia,
disturbing the peace on a tree-lined street.
Three died instantly.

Thrown from the plane
the fourth sat in the center of a circle of fire
burning by slow degrees,
first his legs
then his arms and body.

This time people noticed
as they stopped from shopping,
walking the dog,
eating dinner,
to watch the white light turn to ashes.

Walpurgis Stew

They stir the boiling cauldron
dance round the fire thrice
count their collected ingredients

Thirteen parts requisite:
scent of wilted magnolias
urine from a cat in heat

one eye of dragon
two toads' toes
four ravens' eggs

wart from a newt's nose
red rooster's guts
the horse's hind hoof

Seasoned with a snake's spit
love potion for an ardent admirer
seeking a lover's kiss.

Free Spirits

She looks surprised in the silence
hidden behind locked doors
where no one can harm her
slow to see a bright sunrise
beyond heaven's awning

When he knocks, she opens for his smile
laughing at blue crabs in his hands
the muck rising round his knees
both mired in a quicksand of desire
stolen kisses bruising their bodies.

Sonnet of Delight

When I have fears that my life will end before it has begun
before I know who I am and what I will become
I think of how you know our waking and sleeping
serenely living today, not yesterday or tomorrow

Then I do the same wherever I may wander
feel the sun rise in morning, the moon glow at night
not caring what I wear or how I comb my hair
watching the deer at dark and squirrels in light

Where daisies grow by green willows and streams
I stop to touch the petals, drink the scents of spring
At the winter's snow I freeze to dream of clouds
like angels in white drifting high above our heads

There in a golden mist tinged with blue and pink skies
we kiss, and iridescent fish swim beneath the trees.

Death of Romance

We step barefoot into the snow
stopping only once at the ledge
Our naked bodies burn and roll
melting a fiery path
to far reaches of white lawn

When we stop, I watch him sleeping
curled into a ball, head on his arm
I call his name but he does not answer
till I whisper Romance, Romance, and
for the last time he looks into my eyes.

Spa Night

Bushes shrouded in black plastic
notices tacked on a bulletin board
Kathy's says, "I do hair, especially braids"

At the spa, two new friends and I relax
with a dozen other women
We shalom to the master of exercise

lie prone at his slippered feet
arise at his command, sit along a wall
on a long bench, sheathed in black tights

We wait our turns for flu injections and
a muscular man mounts a robotic horse
offers to show us dolls his tricks

He's from Central America with a romantic twist
smiles, gallops in a sexy manner
We feign disinterest till a new patient arrives

with bottles of wine in a tapestry sack
She's a romantic who offers the owner her hand
which he kisses as they waltz away.

Thunder

I have washed and wiped the dishes
searching through a rain-spotted window
for a breeze, a stirring, some sign

The branches, like black lace
silhouetted against the white sky,
reach beyond the mountains

From a distance, rolling rocks
tumble once more and
the baby stops crying

She now nestles in my lap
the dog a furry ball at our feet
and I yearn for your touch

in the silence.

Comic Strips

I cut a bibbed apron
exactly straight along the edges
from the funny papers
with my silver scissors

The scraps I crumple and
stuff into a bedside drawer
clippings across the floor
hands stained red and gray

I try it on and it fits just right
crinkles as I move around in bed
smells like perfume of printer's ink
tempts me to unknown events

Wearing this smock I sit with a crowd
talk cookies, books and dreams
Their unclear questions attack my brain
like headlines from tomorrow's news

They ask what Tolstoy's teacher wrote
in a note to his mother, my garbled response
something like "going to America"
and they want to know more

Fuzzy dogs jump in and out the folds and
the family circus holds a picnic on my lap
Tourists and baldheaded strangers
envy and admire my papery protector

They thrust dollars at me, want to buy one
For better or worse I remove my apron and sell
In the morning I blink my eyes and snap on the light
run to the porch in pajamas for today's latest decor.

Our Son's Odyssey

In the winter's misty web, we watched
snow falling lightly at Tavern on the Green,
just eating our dinner and drinking our wine,
till our son unfurled his dream.

After quitting his job and selling his car,
he departed on a rainy June day,
temperatures in the eighties,
lightning and thunder above the tarmac.

His web site glowed with Tokyo sunrises
Sumatra sunsets, fluffy chicks dyed red and green,
a golden Buddha in Bali, temples in Thailand
monks in saffron robes, tunnels of Vietnam.

Packages stamped pink and purple appeared
bearing strange tasseled hats of black velvet
shiny sequined elephants on silk purses
golden coins reflecting foreign faces.

Hiking from Nepal to India he met a man
who told him life appears in many forms;
in the Jesuit cathedral of Goa, old priests
toasted a new millennium with incense.

From Turkey to Egypt
Greece Jordan Israel
he touched hands with men and women
snapped photos of smiling children.

One year later, he phoned us from Peru
while waiting for a bus to Brazil,
still carrying a pack on his back,
loaded with souvenirs and stories.

The Way Things Work

I clap my hands to the beat of drums
palms and fingers in steady rhythm
creating degrees of hypnotic sound

They come with no directions
nor manual of operation
no warranties or guarantees

Meant to stroke a kitten's fur
plant and pick flowers
hold onto slippery dreams

Made to swing an axe
turn a page or sign your name
how they work is a mystery

Small soft hands lengthen
once smooth now wrinkled
strangers on the keyboard.

World Trade Center: September 11, 2001

The unspeakable seeks words:
a way to heal
a way to sleep all night
without pills or appetite.

Though words are only words,
they must suffice:
a way to shape the saga
a way to form the future.

The unimaginable act burns towers,
incinerates workers at their desks;
the swirling winds carry ashes
to settle at every door.

Nothing makes sense today,
stories of dark and light jumbled together:
a sculptor killed whose work foretold the future,
leaving us his statue of a man pierced by airplanes.

A dog leads its blind master down countless stairs;
Firemen stop to help an injured woman,
but not all escape the falling debris.
Pets await their owners at apartment windows.

People run toward the water
away from the inferno:
shoeless, hatless, homeless,
searching family.

Within seconds, phones ring round the globe
from cousins, brothers, friends
who seek to know our fate,
whether we are victims or survivors.

Our lives are altered by small or large degrees,
united by yokes of suffering.
Words are merely words, piled one atop each other,
yet with them we can build towers of courage.

Words from Afar

On a small damaged scroll from Hanoi
Zen Buddhist monk
by way of my son
sends painted characters on rice paper
wrapped round a broken bamboo stick
   Countless forms on path of poetry.

Acknowledgments

Grateful acknowledgment is made to the editors of the magazines where the following poems first appeared: "Still Playing Checkers" and "Haying" in *Goldfinch*; "Our Son's Odyssey" in *Off the Coast*; "Half Remembered/Half Forgotten" in *Paterson Literary Review*; "News of the Crash" in *Red River Review*; and "Autumn Dream," "Dogs in the Canary Islands," "Eyes Shut Tight," "Signs along Life's Highway," and "Where I Sleep" in *Stray Dog*.

Some of the poems published in her first book, *Grave Rubbings: New and Selected Poems,* appear in *Riding My Tricycle: Poetry of Dreams and Visions* by the author's permission. They are "Autumn Dream," "Cemetery Cave," "Half Asleep," "The Long Way," "Still Playing Checkers," and "Tractor."

The author thanks Brenda D. Chmiel and Dr. Claire E. Brown for their assistance during the time this book was written. Members of her Morning Muses group, part of the Women Who Write cooperative, also deserve a heartfelt mention for their critiquing and confidence.